BBC MUSIC GUIDES

———

RACHMANINOV ORCHESTRAL MUSIC

BBC MUSIC GUIDES

Rachmaninov Orchestral Music

PATRICK PIGGOTT

UNIVERSITY OF WASHINGTON PRESS
SEATTLE

The music examples are reproduced by kind permission of the following: Belwin-Mills Publishing Corp. for Ex. 3–4; Boosey & Hawkes Music Publishers Ltd for Ex. 8–15, 23–7; Schott & Co. Ltd for Ex. 16–22, 28.

First published 1974 by the British Broadcasting Corporation
Copyright © Patrick Piggott 1974
University of Washington Press edition first published 1974
Library of Congress Catalog Card Number 73-13333
ISBN 0-295-95308-x
Printed in England

Contents

Introduction

Rachmaninov's dual career as composer and pianist has given rise
to a number of misconceptions about him. One of them, still widely
current, is that he was primarily a composer of piano music who
also happened to write some rather good music for other media.
Another misconception is that because he was so pre-eminent as a
virtuoso his orchestral music tended to be pianistic in style – rather
like orchestrated piano music. Liszt, at one time, had to suffer the
same ill-informed criticism. In fact, Rachmaninov's output of solo
piano music, though splendidly written for the instrument, is not
particularly voluminous: two sonatas, two sets of variations, and
between fifty and sixty small pieces are its sum total. On the other
hand, his operas, choral works, songs, chamber music and orchestral music constitute a large and important corpus of work, and in
all these widely different types of music he was quite as much at his
ease as when writing for the piano. It is often forgotten that Rachmaninov, as well as being a composer and a pianist, was a conductor
of exceptional gifts, which he displayed as brilliantly in the opera
house as in the concert hall; that though the rigorous training by
Zverev combined with his own innate talent gave him a prodigious
piano technique at a very early age, his later musical education at
the Moscow Conservatoire was comprehensive and extremely
thorough; and that during his subsequent dazzling career in Russia
he was, while celebrated both as a conductor and a pianist, admired,
above all, as a composer.

Rachmaninov has had to suffer from other misconceptions. One
hears it said that after he left Russia in 1917 and decided, at the late
age of forty-five, to adopt an international virtuoso's career his
creative powers gradually withered away. For this error, it must be
admitted, he is himself partly to blame. His well-known reply to his
friend Medtner, who had asked him why he no longer composed
(one would like to know just *when* Medtner asked him this irritating
question), 'How can I compose when the melody has gone?', has
been quoted too often. In fact 'the melody' (by which one must
suppose he really meant the urge to compose, since the last works
he wrote in Russia, the *Etudes-Tableaux*, Op. 39, are less concerned
with melody than with experiments in texture and sonority and with
the creation of mood) had by no means left him, as the music of his
last decade clearly shows. But legends die hard, and this one has

been sedulously fostered by present-day Russians who prefer to think that without the feel of his native soil under his feet a Russian composer must necessarily lapse into silence. To believe this is to ignore facts, one of which is that, out of the twelve works discussed in this essay, six were composed outside Russia. It also ignores the work of other exiled Russian creative artists – of Alexandre Benois, Vladimir Nabokov, Marc Chagall and Stravinsky, to name a few. And what of Prokofiev (whose works written in exile are by no means inferior to those written after his return to Russia), and of Medtner himself, who went on composing ceaselessly wherever he was, hardly aware of his surroundings? And how could Rachmaninov, with the music of another exile, his beloved Chopin, always in his ears and fingers, seriously believe that it was his separation from his homeland which was preventing him from composing, rather than the fact that he was too busy with his demanding new career as an international virtuoso pianist?

His remarks about his problems as a composer are, furthermore, often contradictory. Sometimes he insisted that he was unfitted to write large symphonies, that never again would he embark on extended orchestral works; but he also complained that to write a small piano piece was the hardest task of all, an absolute torment, and that he found it much easier to write for the orchestra because the mere thought of the varied instrumental colours was in itself an inspiration. It was the same with his piano playing: sometimes he hated it; it was a burden, a drudgery; but when advised to retire for the sake of his health he could not face the thought of life without concerts – they became the very *raison d'être* of his existence. Like many artists, he could be moody, sometimes filled with gloom, at others quite the reverse, as Madame Rachmaninov's recently published reminiscences reveal;[1] and Medtner's tactless enquiry might have had quite a different and perhaps a more bracing reply on another day.

Another extremely inaccurate statement still made about Rachmaninov's music from time to time is that it is 'cosmopolitan' in style – not very Russian in idiom. One of the silliest descriptions of it was written by the late van Loon, who bracketed Rachmaninov's music with that of César Cui as being tinged with 'Westernism' (a pejorative word in the context). How this may apply to Cui, who was, after all, of Belgian descent, need not concern us here, but it is

[1] *Novyi Zhurnal*, no. 103 (New York 1970).

nonsense when applied to Rachmaninov, whose work is deeply rooted in that of Tchaikovsky, Mussorgsky and Rimsky-Korsakov, and, above all, in the traditional music of the Russian Orthodox Church. Ask the contemporary Russian 'man in the street' who goes to concerts what kind of music means most to him, and ten to one he will reply Tchaikovsky and/or Rachmaninov, with the occasional variation of Skryabin (there is an interesting Skryabin cult in Russia). When Stravinsky claimed that Tchaikovsky is the most Russian of all composers he knew very well what he was about: Tchaikovsky's music, for all its apparent universality, is always deeply 'in tune' with the Russian 'soul'. Rachmaninov was, of course, a lesser composer than Tchaikovsky, but his music also touches the Russian heart in a special way and it is revered in his native land for this reason. Not for nothing is Ivanovka, his former country home, now being reconstructed exactly as it was in his day and transformed into a place of pilgrimage, complete with a luxury hotel for the pilgrims! Very soon it will be a national shrine second only to the Tchaikovsky museum at Klin.

But despite his peculiarly Russian musical personality, perhaps even because of it, Rachmaninov, like Tchaikovsky, has a worldwide appeal. An enormous number of letters came to him from every corner of the world, most of them containing touchingly simple expressions of gratitude for the mere existence of the man whose music had so deeply moved the writers. Equally touching was the kindness and tact with which Rachmaninov replied to them, giving up for the purpose precious hours that might have been used for composition. Yet this same music, which has given pleasure to millions, has also received much snubbing criticism over the years and still meets with misunderstanding and even antagonism as well as continued acclamation. The curious dichotomy in critical attitudes to Rachmaninov was recently exemplified by the American writer Eric Salzman, who published simultaneously two articles about him, one entitled 'Da', and the other 'Nyet'.[1] This at least implies that a judgement on the ultimate value of his work remains an open question which we may decide for ourselves. A closer acquaintance with his major works, which include most of those that he wrote for orchestra, will help us to do so.

[1] *Stereo Review*, vol. 30, no. 5 (New York 1973).

Miscellaneous Orchestral Works

Though Rachmaninov's early symphonic poem *The Crag* was the first of his orchestral works to be published, it was by no means his first experiment in writing for the orchestra. From the age of thirteen, when he transcribed for piano duet Tchaikovsky's enormous 'Manfred' Symphony from the then recently published full score (learning a great deal about orchestration in the process), to the age of twenty, when he wrote *The Crag*, no year passed without the composition of one or more orchestral works. There is a Scherzo in F, dating from his fourteenth year; a piano concerto, sketched but not fully worked out; part of a symphonic work based, like Tchaikovsky's symphony, on Byron's 'Manfred', of which at least one movement is known to have been completed; a Suite, now lost; another piano concerto which was to become his Op. 1 and which, in a drastically revised version made many years later, is still part of the pianist's repertoire; an attempt at a Symphony in D minor, of which the first movement still exists; another symphony, said to have been completed but at once discarded; a symphonic poem, *Prince Rostislav,* after a ballad by Alexey Tolstoy; and lastly the opera *Aleko,* which contains some purely orchestral pieces (two dances and an intermezzo). In these works the orchestra is handled with growing certainty, and Rachmaninov must have gained valuable practical experience during the rehearsals and performances of *Aleko* in the spring of 1893.

The Crag shows clearly the benefit of so much practice in orchestration, even though the material on which it is based develops very little and is, in itself, rather vague and tenuous. Still, the work must have been warmly approved by Tchaikovsky, for he actually offered to include it in his programmes during a European tour which he was planning for the winter of 1893, but which, owing to his sudden death in October of that year, never took place.

One wonders what it was about Rachmaninov's piece which so greatly pleased the usually hypercritical composer of the recently completed *Symphonie Pathétique.* Was it merely the obvious affiliation of the youthful composer's style to his own, or did he discern some quality in the work which is no longer evident to us who know the direction in which Rachmaninov's talent was later to develop? Of course, the acid test of the lasting value of a work of art is neither its modernity nor its technique; but when we realise that *The Crag* is an exact contemporary of Debussy's *Prélude à l'après-midi d'un faune* it becomes clear that Rachmaninov, even at the age of twenty, was by no means an *avant-garde* composer; yet Tchaikovsky, who would probably have disapproved of Debussy's iconoclastic piece had he lived to hear it, believed his young protégé to be the man of the future, at least as far as Russian music was concerned. This high opinion he formed on the evidence of Rachmaninov's very early works, of which *The Crag* was the last that he heard.

Perhaps it was the slightly morbid, even rather depressing atmosphere of the work (it faithfully reflects the source of Rachmaninov's inspiration, which is a sad little tale by Chekhov about the chance meeting and subsequent parting of a young girl and a much older man whose ruined life lies behind him) which interested and touched Tchaikovsky and allowed him to excuse certain technical shortcomings which he cannot have failed to observe. There is no doubt that a proper appreciation of Rachmaninov's tone poem is only possible when it is realised that the lines from Lermontov's poem, 'The Crag',

> 'The little golden cloud spent the night
> On the breast of the giant crag',

which he placed at the head of his score, merely symbolise the characters in Chekhov's story: they had actually been used as a prefix to it by Chekhov himself.

Rachmaninov might have been wiser had he been more open about the real meaning of his music, but perhaps he may have felt that Chekhov's affecting tale, when reduced to a mere 'programme note' account of an emotional overnight meeting between two strangers at an inn, would displease the lorgnette-wielding dowagers who ruled Moscow's musical society in the 1890s. It would probably have been equally unacceptable to the late Victorian audience to whom Rachmaninov introduced himself at a Philharmonic Society concert at Queen's Hall in 1899 with a performance of this very work.

Despite Tchaikovsky's good opinion of it, *The Crag* was not then, and has never since been, a resounding success. It was not that people actively disliked it (though the *Musical Times* critic spoke unkindly of its themes 'crawling about in apologetic half-tones'): they merely found it vague and insubstantial, as indeed they still do. The young composer's orchestration cannot be faulted, but he relied too much on the repetition of short phrases which, however often they are refurbished by changes of key, register, tempo and instrumentation, eventually become overworked, if not to their deaths, then certainly to a very exhausted condition. However, the gloomy opening theme, played by cellos and basses, is not given this treatment: its only reappearance is reserved for the climax of the whole work, where it rings out in brazen grandeur through the rich scoring for full orchestra. This short theme and another later motif melodically related to it (also allotted to the bass strings) seem to symbolise the tragic figure of the man in Chekhov's story (the 'Crag' of Lermontov's poem), whereas a delicate, arpeggio-like figure which trips up and down in ornamental arabesques for the woodwind, as well as another charmingly scored little episode featuring a solo flute, probably symbolises the 'Cloud', the young girl in Chekhov's story who listens, at first with little interest, but later with increasing emotion, to the man's sad life-story.

The first of these 'feminine' motifs is heard far more often than it deserves, but this miscalculation is slight compared with the treatment of what soon proves to be the principal theme of the work, a little two-bar phrase

Ex. 1

out of which Rachmaninov tries to develop a romantically emotional theme in Tchaikovsky's style, complete with woodwind solos, soaring strings and lavish accompaniments. But he succeeds only in producing a chain of repetitions, relieved occasionally by an equally short-breathed answering phrase. It is the failure of this part of the work which is its greatest weakness: Rachmaninov is as if hypnotised by his *petite phrase*, which seems to have had for him some positively Proustian significance at the time, for he was still under its spell when he composed his next work, the Trio, Op. 9, written in memory of Tchaikovsky, in which the same phrase appears, robbed of its chromatic inflections but nevertheless clearly recognisable in the opening bars of the theme of the variation movement.

In 1908 Rachmaninov, in a letter to his friend Nikita Morozov, mentioned that he often worried about three of his early works: the First Concerto, the First Symphony and the *Capriccio on gypsy themes,* Op. 12. 'How I should like,' he wrote, 'to see all of these in corrected, decent form.' He did not include *The Crag* in this private list, but this does not necessarily mean that he remained unaware of its shortcomings. Probably, like many composers, he placed little value on most of his early music (he refused to attend the New York performances of *Aleko* in 1925) but regarded the three compositions he mentioned as more in need of 'rescue-work' than the others. Just how brilliantly he could transform early material can be seen in the 1917 revision of his First Concerto. Unfortunately he never found time to rewrite any of his other early works in the same way, and *The Crag* remains as he first composed it —efficiently scored, obviously indebted to Tchaikovsky (though not without a few characteristic turns of phrase), reflecting with fair accuracy the sense of frustration and sorrow as well as some of the tenderness of the Chekhov story which provided Rachmaninov with his secret programme, but too indefinite thematically to earn it more than an occasional revival today as an interesting curiosity.

CAPRICCIO ON GYPSY THEMES, OP. 12

One should not be misled by the alternative title, *Capriccio Bohémien,* under which this work occasionally appears in programmes, and which was even printed on the title page of the first edition. The French word *Bohémien* certainly means 'gypsy', but it has other meanings as well; and it should be understood that the *Capriccio* has no more to do with Bohemia, the native land of Smetana and Dvořák, than it has with the 'Bohemians' of Murger's novel or Puccini's opera *La Bohème*. The Russian title, which describes the Capriccio as *na tziganskiye temyi* (on gypsy themes), makes this perfectly clear.

Though conceived from the first as an orchestral piece, the work was initially written as a piano duet and orchestrated some time later. The name of its dedicatee, Pyotr Lodyzhensky, explains the composer's use of gypsy themes as his material, for Lodyzhensky's wife Anna was a woman of gypsy origin. To her Rachmaninov had already dedicated his first published song, and her initials were to appear on the score of his First Symphony, the work on which he embarked shortly after completing the *Capriccio*.

It may as well be admitted at once that though it is effectively scored, the *Capriccio on gypsy themes* is not one of Rachmaninov's important pieces. It contains so few recognisable characteristics of his style – fewer even than the earlier tone-poem *The Crag* – that it would be difficult to guess its composer's name. Writing to his friend Mikhail Slonov in July 1894, Rachmaninov mentioned that he had already completed the piano duet version of the work, but added that he wanted to look through some scores by other composers before attempting its instrumentation. The success of such pieces as Rimsky-Korsakov's dazzling *Capriccio Espagnol* and Tchaikovsky's almost equally brilliant *Capriccio Italien* may have prompted the young composer to try his hand at an orchestral fantasia similarly based on folk melodies, and probably these were among the works he studied before orchestrating his own. But though its scoring is certainly its best feature, Rachmaninov's *Capriccio* cannot compete with its famous forerunners in virtuosity and vividness of colouring. It also differs from them in form; for whereas Tchaikovsky and Rimsky-Korsakov adopted a design similar to that of Liszt's *Hungarian Rhapsodies,* in which strongly contrasted material is set in kaleidoscopic juxtaposition, Rachmaninov builds his substantial work out of a few short, pithy motifs common to all sections of the piece, sometimes developing them symphonically and sometimes treating them more in the manner of free variations. The conception is good in itself, and had it been carried out more convincingly it might have resulted in an interestingly fresh approach to the folkloric fantasia popular with most Russian composers since the time of Glinka. But the *Capriccio* gives the impression of having been written too hurriedly. The gypsy themes are not particularly striking in themselves (were they, perhaps, in some way associated with the Lodyzhensky family?), and their treatment is rather conventional. This is a drawback for which the resourceful orchestration cannot fully compensate the listener. In later years Rachmaninov regretted the publication of this score. In a letter written in 1908 he said that the thought of it 'frightened' him, and that he hoped to find time to revise it. Unfortunately he never did.

The *Capriccio* is in the key of E and falls into three distinct sections. The first begins with what is in many ways the most striking passage in the whole work: an introduction in which a continuous, throbbing drum rhythm provides a background against which fragments of a dance motif are introduced, slowly at first, but with mounting speed and excitement until a brilliant climax erupts. At this point the drum rhythm is transferred to the tambourine, an instrument traditionally associated with gypsies. This stormy episode blows itself out as quickly as it arises, and the music gradually reverts to the gloomy orchestral colouring of the opening, the soft, agitated drumming fading at last into silence. So far so good. But now occurs what is, perhaps, a miscalculation; for having based his introduction on a tonic pedal, Rachmaninov continues to use this device throughout the greater part of the first section of the work. It underlies the whole of the *lento lugubre, alla marcia funebre* which immediately follows the introduction and moves with a slow, dragging step on every second beat (it is in 3/4 time), while the entire string orchestra, less the double-basses, pours out a melody of passionate lamentation. This theme, with its chromatically wailing inflections, is derived from the dance motif hinted at in the introduction, and no sooner have the strings abandoned it than it is taken up by a solo clarinet, delicately supported by the violins (tremolando and pizzicato) and curiously adorned with faint jingling sounds from the triangle and tambourine. The tonic pedal has already begun to outstay its welcome, but it continues throughout the clarinet's solo, and even when the key changes for the appearance of a new theme, allotted to the flute, the bass adheres to the note E (now the mediant of C sharp minor) throughout the greater part of the flute's tender, pathetic melody. Only in its concluding phrases is the pedal device, omnipresent until this point, relinquished to allow for a series of cadential phrases in the new key.

There follows an *andante molto sostenuto*; and here, freed at last from the anchor of a pedal bass, the music begins to roam throughout a wide range of keys in an extensive development of motifs taken from the flute melody. This central part of the *Capriccio* is charged with a more personal emotion than the rest of the work (it is the one section in which the youthful Rachmaninov's style is recognisable), and it reaches a passionate climax where pulsating violin rhythms are set against sombre reminiscences of the gypsy lament, played here by trumpets and trombones. The *andante* ends with two passages for solo cello which recall the opening of the flute theme. These sad cello phrases are interrupted, first by clarinets and then by oboes, with what proves to be an anticipation of the main theme of the final section, a lively dance motif in thirds that lacks any noticeable gypsy flavour (it seems typically Russian in idiom) but is treated in a way which is obviously meant to represent the wild abandon of the playing of the gypsy bands that were so popular in the Russia of Rachmaninov's youth. The dance finale is scored in an appropriately colourful manner, but the constant reiteration of its few short phrases, nearly always presented in thirds or sixths and invariably in the upper part of the orchestral texture, betrays the composer's inexperience in handling this sort of material. Apart from the four-bar phrase with which it begins, the themes are mostly derived from the 'lament' and the flute melody; but there is one new motif, a little 'oriental' arabesque, which adds a touch of the exotic (very much *à propos* in the context) and provides an occasion for the use of 'barbaric' open fifths and for some effective unprepared key changes. The arabesque figure makes a brief but impressive final appearance in a short *grave* passage which momentarily interrupts the vertiginous dance movement before a *prestissimo* coda brings the *Capriccio* to a suitably rousing conclusion.

THE ISLE OF THE DEAD, OP. 29

Like the music of Debussy (with most of which, however, he was out of sympathy), Rachmaninov's instrumental works were frequently the outcome of a stimulus received from painting or literature. He was usually reticent about such sources of inspiration, preferring to publish his music without evocative titles. In this he was wise; for whereas it is improbable that his unsuccessful First Piano Sonata would have fared better had it been published as 'A Faust Sonata' (it follows an undisclosed programme similar to that of Liszt's 'Faust' Symphony), the public's ignorance of the pictorial inspiration behind, for instance, the splendid Prelude in B minor, Op. 32, no. 10, has not hindered that piece from being recognised as one of Rachmaninov's finest achievements.

In later years Rachmaninov liked to use the title *Etude-Tableau* for his smaller works, and this may be regarded as a partial admission that many of them are based on pictorial ideas; but the only mature composition which, he openly avowed, had a direct connection with the work of another artist is the symphonic poem *The Isle of the*

Dead, inspired by Arnold Böcklin's once-famous painting of that name.

Rachmaninov was at the height of his powers when in 1909 he wrote this work, which is undoubtedly one of his masterpieces. Its subject is, of course, ideally suited to him (one cannot imagine that he would have made an equal success of a musical interpretation of Böcklin's companion picture 'The Isle of the Living'). He once stated, in a letter to the Armenian poetess Marietta Shaginian, that he preferred subjects that were sad rather than cheerful. 'Light, gay colours,' he wrote, 'do not come easily to me.' In Böcklin's gloomy, atmospheric picture he found everything he needed: sombre shadows; a sense of the presence of death and of the mysteries beyond it; even the suggestion of a striking and unusual rhythm, ready made for him, in the slow, regular dipping of Charon's oars as he ferries the departing soul over the dark waters of the Styx on the start of its journey into the unknown. But the suggestive power of Rachmaninov's music carries the listener into regions of the imagination far beyond the range of the Swiss painter's art, and it must be emphasised that it was not so much the quality of Böcklin's painting which stimulated Rachmaninov as its subject.

One must naturally give Böcklin the credit for the vision which led him to transform Pondikonisi[1] – a tiny island off the shores of Corfu, on which stands a chapel within a cypress grove which was once a favourite sanctuary of the ill-fated Empress Elizabeth of Austria – into the mysterious, mythical 'Insel der Toten' of his imagination; but because Rachmaninov was the greater artist of the two his poem transcends the painter's work, not only in the beauty of its detail but in its fantasy and depth of feeling. An additional attraction which the subject – indeed any subject connected with death – had for Rachmaninov was the opportunity it gave him to make use of the 'Dies irae' theme, the old plainsong funeral chant which has had a great fascination for composers since Berlioz showed them what could be done with it in his *Symphonie Fantastique* (see Ex. 2, overleaf).

It was probably the visits of Berlioz to Russia, particularly that of 1867, which first introduced the Russian composers to the apparently endless possibilities of this chant, though Liszt's *Totentanz* variations on the same theme also made a considerable

[1] Some authorities maintain that it was really the island of Ponza, chief of the Pontine Islands in the Tyrrhenian Sea, which was Böcklin's model.

Ex. 2

impression on them. Among the many composers who subsequently used the chant as a musical symbol for death have been Tchaikovsky (several times), Respighi, and, more recently, Shostakovich and Dallapiccola. But none of them used it more frequently than did Rachmaninov.

The chants of the Russian Orthodox Church had an important influence on Rachmaninov's melodic style from his earliest years, but the 'Dies irae' theme, though it belongs to the Roman Catholic and not to the Orthodox ritual, meant even more to him. In *The Isle of the Dead* he uses it with great discretion: it is never stated in full, yet its influence pervades the work throughout. At first, however, the music does no more than suggest the slow dip and pull of Charon's oars, an effect achieved by the use of a rhythm of five quavers to the bar, usually divided ♫ ♫♩, though sometimes this division is reversed. The key is A minor, the tempo *lento,* and for a long time a sustained tonic pedal underlies the undulating motif which, emerging from the cellos, is the principal unifying element in the whole work. A first hint of the 'Dies irae' is heard when its three opening notes are played by a solo horn against the 5/8 rhythm. It is curious that though Rachmaninov never quotes more than a few notes of the theme his music is so filled with a sense of solemn mourning that, even if we were ignorant of the work's connection with Böcklin's picture, we should probably have no difficulty in recognising it to be prompted by images similar to those which inspired D. H. Lawrence's moving poem 'The Ship of Death'.

Having begun by translating the atmosphere of Böcklin's picture into musical terms Rachmaninov shows with what mastery he is now able to develop his material. With little more than the 'rowing' figure of the opening, a few notes from the 'Dies irae' and a variety of rhythmic patterns based on rising and falling chromatic scales, he builds up a powerful symphonic structure in which the occasional intoning, in solemn brass chords, of the 'Dies irae' phrase introduces an awesome sense of impending revelation. Much of the harmony is tied to long-held pedal notes, and the orchestral emphasis is on the lower registers and darker colours. But gradually, as a great climax rises towards the key of E minor, the music bursts into towering heights of sound above the listener – as if it were indeed the great timbered cliffs of Böcklin's visionary island. Then, as the tension relaxes, one becomes aware that the Styx has been crossed, that Charon has shipped his oars, and that the boat is coasting quietly towards the place and the moment when its ghostly passenger must leave it and pass through the final gateway into the unknown. Here the music becomes even more imaginative: the boat glides to its mooring; there is a last warning echo of the 'Dies irae', and then, as the dark cypress grove is entered, there comes a passionate outburst which expresses the departing spirit's last reluctant farewell to the earthly joys and sorrows it is leaving for ever.

Rachmaninov rises splendidly to this very difficult and testing moment with one of the most poignant lyrical passages in all his music: a long, glowing melody in E flat, scored at first only for the upper strings and woodwind, but, as the music increases in tension and complexity, becoming enormously amplified in texture and sonority. The composer, in a letter to Leopold Stokowski, one of his finest interpreters, described how he wished this passage to be played:

It should be a great contrast to all the rest of the work – faster, more nervous and more emotional – as that [sic] passage does not belong to the 'picture', it is in reality a 'supplement' to the picture – which fact makes the contrast all the more necessary. In the former is death – in the latter is life.

Such an intensity of emotion, difficult as it is to express in music, is even harder to sustain for long. Furthermore the demands of musical form cannot be left out of account. It is only to be expected, therefore, that a climactic point will soon be reached at which the familiar 'Dies irae' motif will make a dramatic reappearance (in 1909 one could still make unashamed use of the diminished seventh chord for such an effect), bringing with it the element of recapitulation. From this moment it is the composer's craft which dictates the form of the composition, and matters of musical symbolism become of secondary importance. The 'Dies irae' motif and the 'theme of life' battle desperately together; there is a final, and even more hectic, climax, followed by an extraordinary passage in which the words 'Dies irae' seem to be muttered by a host of mysterious voices. Then, as the departing spirit casts a last wistful, backward glance at the 'theme of life', Charon takes up his oars (here the 5/8 rhythm returns) and slowly re-crosses the Styx, leaving the Isle of the Dead to fade through the shrouding mists of legend into invisibility.

SYMPHONIC DANCES, OP. 45

On 21 August 1940 Rachmaninov wrote to Eugene Ormandy, offering him the first performance of a new work which he had just composed and which he then called 'Fantastic Dances'. At that time the orchestration had not been completed, but before the last touches had been put to the score Rachmaninov had changed the title to *Symphonic Dances*. Though it was to be his last work, this music by the sixty-eight-year-old composer is as vigorous as any of his earlier compositions. It is scored with an effectiveness at least equal to that of his other late works, and while it does not possess the opulent romanticism many people associate with his music, its first two movements both contain long-breathed melodies which are distinctive and haunting. Rachmaninov's original intention had been to give the three dances titles – *Mid-day*, *Twilight* and *Midnight* – and, with the success of the balletic version of the Paganini Rhapsody in mind, he invited the choreographer, Mikhail Fokine, to hear the new work even before he had introduced it to Ormandy. Fokine's reactions to the music, as played by Rachmaninov on the piano, were, as one might expect, flatteringly enthusiastic, but he was non-committal about its choreographic possibilities, and Rachmaninov never saw his work staged. Later he denied that he had ever had any ideas of a ballet in mind while composing it, and certainly, despite the central waltz movement, the work is essentially symphonic.

It was Rachmaninov's sensible habit to ask a professional string player to check the bowing of the string parts of his scores before they were printed. He usually asked his old colleague of Moscow days, Julius Conus, to undertake this task for him, but in the case of the *Symphonic Dances*, as Rachmaninov proudly told Ormandy, the bowings were done by none other than Fritz Kreisler. The difficulties of which string players sometimes complain when they encounter this work have nothing to do with the fact that it happens to be by one of the greatest of all piano virtuosi, but because the strings parts were edited by one of the greatest of violin virtuosi.

The first movement, which is full of rhythmic drive and subtle orchestral colouring (including the discreet use of a piano, mostly as a percussion instrument), begins with a march-like theme whose most immediately striking figure is the descending triad with which it opens:

Ex. 3

This figure, in various forms, is the basis of nearly all the thematic material of the first section, and is also an important feature of the long, expressive melody allotted to the saxophone in the central episode. The saxophone has had a respectable history as an orchestral instrument since Bizet introduced it into his *L'Arlésienne* music, but it was an innovation for Rachmaninov, and he went to considerable pains to ensure that he used the right member of the saxophone family. The alto saxophone's peculiar 'vox humana' timbre ideally suits the theme, and the very spare accompaniment (a single moving part divided between clarinet and oboe) does not detract from its effect.

In addition to the marching theme and the saxophone melody, with its overtones of Russian folk music, there is another important motif, first heard in energetic staccato chords, which seems to contain an echo of a score which was a great favourite of Rachmaninov's, Rimsky-Korsakov's opera *The Golden Cockerel*. He studied this score's orchestration assiduously during his later years and, apart from its clarifying effect on his own style of instrumentation, the well-known chromatic sequences of the Queen of Shemakha's music may well have been the origin of the striking passage in Ex. 4, overleaf.

From this material Rachmaninov constructed a taut and vital piece which, though it is not in classical symphonic form, is truly symphonic in style. It also contains an interesting connection with his First Symphony, a key work in Rachmaninov's early life which, as we shall see, was the cause of much sorrow and disappointment to him. The coda of the first Symphonic Dance ends with a quotation of the motto theme from the symphony, metamorphosed from its original dark, vengeful character to a resigned, sunset glow in C major. It should be realised that the First Symphony

Ex. 4

was still unknown to the world when Rachmaninov penned this passage, and that it must, therefore, have had for him a private, symbolic significance which he did not expect to be recognised by other ears.

The principal theme of the second Symphonic Dance has the character of a *Valse triste*, though it is no miniature dance scene *à la* Sibelius, but an extended fantasy in which slowly gyrating waltz melodies mingle with a strange atmosphere of oppressive anxiety. Even the introductory bars, in which stopped horns and muted trumpets combine in sinister, minatory chords, remind us that the twilight hour can be one of danger. The principal waltz melody is announced by the strings in octaves, preceded by eerie woodwind arabesques which are a feature of the piece and help to create its uneasy mood. The warning brass chords reappear, but as the dance goes on a more romantic feeling gradually eases the tension. Soon, however, all sorts of rhythmic complexities set in, and though the pensive waltz melody is heard again the piece, after rising to a feverish, almost hysterical climax, ends unexpectedly with a curious, fluttering rush of sound. It is as if the dancers had suddenly abandoned the ballroom and disappeared into the surrounding shadows.

In the third Symphonic Dance Rachmaninov turns for the last time to two of his favourite sources of inspiration – the music of the Russian Orthodox Church and the 'Dies irae'. A perceptive critic of the first performance described the piece as a *Danse macabre* (it is, perhaps, relevant that Rachmaninov had added Liszt's *Totentanz* to his repertoire during the previous season), though a journalist with different ideas thought that its rhythmic novelty might possibly have been stimulated by the sound of American dance music. But Rachmaninov's occasional tendency to contort his material into irreverently syncopated variants was not a new departure; there are examples of it in the Fourth Piano Concerto, the Paganini Rhapsody, the Third Symphony and even in such early music as the finale of the First Symphony. In addition to thematic motifs obviously derived from Orthodox chants and from the much-quoted 'Dies irae' there is other material in this piece, some of it dark, even morbid, in mood, some of it more relaxed and romantic. But these passages, though they have their value in the formal scheme, eventually give place to a final long and exhilarating dance in which yet another chant is now introduced, and this eventually dominates the music, triumphing even over the motif of death. It was at the point where this chant first appears, twenty-six bars from the end of the work, that Rachmaninov wrote in his manuscript score the significant word 'Alliluya'[1] (in Latin, not in Cyrillic script). Whether he placed it there as a symbol of the triumph of God over death or as a personal expression of thankfulness at having been able to bring to a successful conclusion this important work, which he may instinctively have felt might be his last (as indeed it was), we cannot know.

Like most of Rachmaninov's later music, the *Symphonic Dances* had to suffer some initial neglect and misunderstanding, but they have now won a place in the orchestral repertoire and are recognised as a masterly example of their composer's later style.

The Symphonies

SYMPHONY NO. 1 IN D MINOR, OP. 13

Rachmaninov's First Symphony was considered for many years to be one of music's shipwrecks. First performed in 1897, it proved a disastrous failure and at once sank to the nether depths of musical history. For over forty years the possibility that it might one day be salvaged was not even considered, for the composer was thought to have destroyed it. In fact the original full score was left behind at his country house when he went into exile in 1917, and though all trace of it seems to have disappeared it may yet come to light. In

[1] Rachmaninov's spelling.

a letter to a friend, written shortly after the first performance, he insisted that though he realised the symphony needed considerable revision he still believed in it: indeed, as late as 1908 he was still hoping to find time to revise it. But Rachmaninov never did revise his First Symphony, and it was not until two years after his death that, the original orchestral parts having been accidentally found in the library of the Leningrad Conservatoire, a new score was compiled so that the symphony could be revived. It had its second performance in 1945.

On hearing this interesting and romantic, if not wholly satisfactory, symphony today one realises that the original first performance must have been indescribably bad. On that occasion it was conducted by Alexander Glazunov, and according to the memoirs of Rachmaninov's friend Alfred Swan, Madame Rachmaninov maintained that Glazunov was drunk at the time. Rachmaninov discreetly made no mention of this in the letter which he sent to A. V. Zatayevich shortly after the performance, although he wrote:

I am amazed – how can a man with the great talent of Glazunov conduct so badly? I speak not merely of his conducting technique (useless to expect that of him) but of his musicianship. He feels nothing while he conducts – it is as if he understands nothing!

Obviously the performance must have been a travesty such as even a less difficult and experimental symphony could not have survived. Unfortunately the psychological effect on the young composer was extremely wounding and prolonged, and it was fully three years before he recovered confidence in his creative ability.

Even if the symphony had been given an adequate first performance it is unlikely that it would have pleased the St Petersburg public, never very favourably disposed towards the younger representatives of the Moscow school, for Rachmaninov really did try to open up new paths by making considerable use of motifs derived from the *Octeochos,* the ancient chants of the Russian Orthodox Church. It is sometimes assumed that the symphony is entirely based on these chants, but what Rachmaninov did was to take small melodic cells from the *Octeochos* and weld them into themes suitable for symphonic development. The same few motifs are used in all four movements of the symphony, and they give it a unity which is certainly a virtue, though the listener is inclined to tire of them before the end is reached.

Not all the themes, however, are derived from the formulas of

Russian church music. The second subject of the first movement, for instance, has a chromatic, quasi-oriental character far removed from the diatonicism of the *Octeochos* chants. It has been suggested that this theme was deliberately composed in something like the so-called 'gypsy' scale (the harmonic minor scale with a sharpened fourth) as a reference to the symphony's dedicatee, Anna Lodyzhenskaya, a woman of gypsy origin who was married to one of Rachmaninov's friends. Actually the theme is not really in the 'gypsy' scale, and the hints made by romantic biographers that the young Rachmaninov was perhaps in love with Madame Lodyzhenskaya should be ignored. It is true that the composer placed at the head of his score the biblical epigraph, 'Vengeance is mine, I will repay', and that this same epigraph was used by Lev Tolstoy for *Anna Karenina,* which (among a great many other things) tells the sad story of a love affair between a young man and a beautiful older woman; but this does not mean that the symphony is an autobiographical document, *à la* Berlioz, with Rachmaninov seeing himself in the role of Count Vronsky and Madame Lodyzhenskaya (who, incidentally, was a confirmed invalid) in the role of Anna. That the work has a hidden programme is quite possible, for Rachmaninov was given to literary sources of inspiration; but as the epigraph is the only clue we have it is much better considered on its musical merits and defects alone and not as an excuse for romantic fantasies.

The symphony opens with a tiny melodic germ, no more than an inverted turn, which acts both as a preface to the main theme and also as a motto for the whole work. It is convenient to call it the 'vengeance' motif (*a*):

Ex. 5

It is easy to hear in the phrase which completes the short introduction (*b*) the sound of a solemn ecclesiastical chant, but one will look in vain among the thousands of chants which form the *Octeochos* for one which is shaped in exactly this way. Its narrow intervals are typical of all such chants, and they are also to be found in many of Rachmaninov's other works, for the influence on his music of traditional Russian church music extends far beyond the First Symphony. This striking phrase is immediately transformed into the principal subject of the *allegro*. The short motif in the lower strings which overlaps the last notes of the main theme should also be noted. Though at a first glance there seems to be nothing ecclesiastical about it, the passage marked (*c*) is to be found in many of the *Octeochos* chants. As the piece develops it has an increasingly important part to play:

Ex. 6

Allegro ma non troppo

Mention has already been made of the strongly contrasted second subject, with its languorously chromatic and exotic character. Yet in the midst of its sensuous, caressing phrases a little swaying rhythm appears (*d*), which may also be traced to the *Octeochos*. This rhythm recurs in many other parts of the work:

Ex. 7

Meno mosso

The development section begins with a lively fugue on a subject derived from a combination of (*b*) and (*c*), and it reaches its climax with a thrilling version of (*b*) on trombones and tuba, accompanied by slashing pizzicato chords, spiky woodwind quavers and the rhythm ♩ ♫ ♩ ♫ on horns, bassoons and clarinets. This marching rhythm is a typical Rachmaninov 'fingerprint'. At the crucial point where the composer must find a convincing link between this last, exciting transformation of his themes and their recapitulation in their original forms he turns to a formula which had been available to Russian composers since Glinka first used it in *Ruslan* – the whole-tone scale. And from here it is a fairly easy transition to the original key and to an impressive restatement of the introductory motifs.

The recapitulation follows much the same lines as the exposition, though with changed dynamics and scoring. But there is an interesting addition to it in the use of the 'vengeance' motif as an internal counterpoint to the main theme. In the unusual ending to the movement the ever-closer rhythmic compression of the principal theme has the effect of finally crushing it into silence.

The Scherzo begins with a very short introduction consisting of (*a*) on muted violas followed by (*d*) on muted second violins. The principal theme follows immediately. It is a simple four-bar phrase in thirds which is later inverted, the two phrases being separated by animated figures of which the main feature is a little three-note horn call. Out of this slender material the bulk of the Scherzo is built. The main theme, obviously derived from the fatalistic chant theme of the first movement, is by no means typical Scherzo material; in fact the whole movement follows an unusual course, for it contains no contrasting Trio. Instead there is a long central section which derives mostly from the first movement's themes, prominence being given to the 'vengeance' motif. There is a harshness both in the scoring and the handling of the material which, one fears, is caused less by intention than by clumsiness. Rachmaninov would surely have rewritten this passage had he revised the symphony. Yet this very music has been admiringly quoted as a prophetic anticipation of Shostakovich (whose music it does not in the least resemble), a comparison which would certainly be unacceptable to both composers. It may have been the Scherzo more than any other part of the symphony which provoked Cui's violent attack on the work as one which 'would enchant all the inmates of Hell'. This was the only occasion in his long career when Rachmaninov was accused of being an advanced modernist.

It is likely that Rachmaninov would have made considerable changes to the slow movement. This *Larghetto* contains, it is true, one of the most romantically beautiful melodies in all his work, but it also includes an inept middle section in which the 'vengeance' motif and fragments of other themes combine to form a gloomy but unmemorable bass theme for strings accompanied by chords for the brass – a passage which even the most careful performance does not save from banality. The movement opens with an introduction which is almost identical with that of the Scherzo: then a solo clarinet sings the beautiful main theme which, when it reappears later in the movement, is rescored with an added counterpoint for two solo cellos. The whole of the last part of the piece is imbued with a peaceful beauty, which is partly achieved by the use of a long tonic pedal, a device much beloved of all Russian composers. Unfortunately the uncomfortable middle section, the rather angular cello counterpoint to the reprise of the main theme and certain other weaknesses prevent this movement from being completely successful despite the great beauty of its principal melody.

The last movement of the symphony contains some of the best music and, for its date, is very advanced in style. After a short introduction based on a new and violently scored version of the 'vengeance' motif, a trumpet fanfare sets the scene for the entry of a festive, extremely Russian theme which is derived in part from the chant motifs of the first movement, now set in new relationships with one another. There is a ferocity and a rhythmic freedom about this *allegro con fuoco* which Rachmaninov did not recapture until the works of his final period and which relate it to his last composition, the third Symphonic Dance, written over forty years later. It makes one wonder how his style might have developed if the symphony had been well played and sympathetically received when it was first performed. The movement also boasts a soaring string melody which helps rather than impedes the music's forward impulse. It is the more regrettable, therefore, that the young composer's determination to knit his symphony together as tightly as possible by a close adherence to the principles of cyclic form induced him to include extended references to themes, and often to whole passages, from earlier movements which are then forced into awkward conjunction with one another. Even if Rachmaninov had been able to carry out this plan with more technical expertise it would have been a precarious undertaking, but in fact his inexperience shows very clearly in the crude scoring and patchwork juxtaposition of the themes in this section. It is a relief when the *allegro con fuoco* reasserts itself and impatiently brushes aside these meandering reminiscences.

The music now leads to a huge climax followed by a short, dramatic silence and then to the symphony's peroration – a grandiose *largo* which, though perhaps a little obvious in its insistence on the ultimate triumph of the 'vengeance' motif, is effectively built up and scored in a suitably impressive manner. Rachmaninov introduces the doom-laden thunder of the tam-tam (a sound he had sensibly held in reserve until this moment) into the concluding pages of the symphony.

One of the more reliable of contemporary critics, Nikolai Findeisen, writing of the first performance,[1] claimed that he saw in Rachmaninov's symphony the evidence of great talent, despite its

[1] *Russkaya Muzykal'naya Gazeta,* April 1897.

weaknesses, and found in the first movement and in what he called 'the furious finale', with its concluding *largo*, 'beauty, novelty and inspiration'. That he was able to detect these qualities in spite of the appallingly bad performance showed great perception, but Findeisen's judgement, lost as it was in the chorus of denunciation from all the other St Petersburg critics, could do little to salve the wounds of the unfortunate young composer, whose previously successful career had not prepared him for an outstanding failure. The echoes of it were to sound in his memory for many years to come.

SYMPHONY NO. 2 IN E MINOR, OP. 27

Ten years separate Rachmaninov's first completed symphony from his second, but in those ten years he had won world-wide fame with his numerous and very popular piano pieces and songs and, above all, with his Second Concerto.

In Moscow, where he occupied a very prominent place in the musical world, he was beginning to feel somewhat hindered by the near-impossibility of finding time to compose, so great were the demands made on him. In the winter of 1906, therefore, he decided to leave Russia, if only temporarily, and settle in Dresden. To live almost incognito seemed now the only way to compose without interruption. He was particularly anxious to write a great symphony which would surpass even the success of the Second Concerto and (more important) finally erase the memories, which still rankled, o the First Symphony's failure.

In a large measure he succeeded. Rachmaninov's Second Symphony, composed in Dresden in 1907, is one of his best and most characteristic works. It is long (an enthusiastic critic, writing of the first performance, noted the audience's unflagging attention throughout the symphony's sixty-five minutes), but its thematic material is strong and varied and handled with mastery, and the orchestration, though neither subtle nor unusual, is always appropriate. The symphony's length has been criticised, and it is still often performed with savage cuts which sometimes reduce its overall length by as much as twenty minutes. The composer himself set an unfortunate precedent by making cuts in his own works, but the fluctuations of fashion having brought the large-scale romantic symphony back into popular favour, the public which now delights in the symphonies of Bruckner, Mahler and Elgar would scarcely jib at an hour of Rachmaninov in his most uninhibitedly emotional mood. Unfortunately old habits cling tightly, and conductors (perhaps influenced sometimes by cuts already pencilled into their hired scores) rarely allow us to hear the Second Symphony as it was originally composed, which is a pity, for in the case of this work form and content are pretty evenly matched.

The first page of the symphony is partly a reworking of an old idea. In 1891, while still a student, Rachmaninov had composed the first movement of a Symphony in D minor (not to be confused with his Op. 13). The score still exists, and in some respects the opening of this forgotten student exercise is strikingly similar to that of the Symphony in E minor. Both begin with a sombre motif in the bass strings followed by rich wind harmonies and a flowing, descending figure for the violins. Here the likeness ends, for the actual thematic material is quite different, as is the mastery with which it is treated. But it seems likely that the opening of this early essay returned to Rachmaninov's mind (doubtless subconsciously) when he sat down in his Dresden studio to begin work on his new symphony.

Like its predecessor, the Second Symphony begins with a motto theme which recurs throughout the whole work and which, with its step-wise movement, might similarly be derived from a Russian Orthodox Church chant. But the motto here (*a*) is expanded into a *largo* of sixty-eight bars and introduces an *allegro moderato*, of which the main theme (*b*) proves to be derived from the motto theme itself (*a*):

Ex. 8 *(a)*

The romantic sadness of this long melody, given to the violins, and the warm lyricism of the beautiful second subject (Ex. 9, opposite) are set off by an animated connecting link featuring vigorous triplet patterns, all these elements being skilfully woven into a tex-

Ex. 9

ture of great luxuriance. To be sure, it is somewhat thickly orchestrated, with frequent doubling of parts that might have been left unsupported had the work been scored by, say, Tchaikovsky, whose influence on Rachmaninov's symphony is more evident in its passionate climaxes than in its instrumentation, which is, at times, of a positively Straussian opulence. In later years Rachmaninov greatly clarified his orchestral style.

The Scherzo which follows is a movement of great vigour and brilliance. It has something of the character of a festive march, and in spite of the fact that the first theme, announced at the outset by the horns, suggests the 'Dies irae' which haunts many of Rachmaninov's principal works, its general mood is one of animation and even gaiety. The horn theme is answered by an important violin motif with a rising figure in it which is later to be transformed into the opening of the finale:

Ex. 10

There is another very important theme in this movement: a romantic, glowing string melody which, moving almost entirely by step, as do so many of Rachmaninov's most memorable themes, seems to be spun from a skein of melody that is apparently endless. But the composer knows exactly when to recall that the business of a Scherzo is not really amorous dalliance (for which there will be ample opportunity later in the slow movement): so, as the violins roam romantically up into the dizziest heights of their E-strings, he allows the woodwind and horns to intrude and gently lead the listener back to a new treatment of the vivid marching music of the Scherzo's opening. Soon there is a feeling that an important goal has been reached – that we are about to witness a significant event.

One wonders what mystery will be unveiled for us; at what celebration shall we assist? What happens may perhaps be compared to a juggling display of great skill; for, with a sudden flash of light, the strings rush forward, tossing glittering variants of the main theme to and fro and gradually drawing the whole orchestra into a whirling fugato. And now a procession of revelling maskers seems to make its way through the flurry of sound. This vision quickly fades, but the jugglery continues with increasing speed until the horns, assisted now by trombones, interrupt its activity with an emphatic restatement of their opening theme in its original form and tempo. The last part of the movement is largely a repetition of the first, but with the addition of a coda in which the disappearing marchers are twice stopped in their tracks by the minatory sound of the brass softly intoning the motto theme of the symphony. This last-minute reference to the motto probably had no specific symbolic significance but was merely a bow in the direction of Tchaikovsky, whose own use of motto themes in his Fourth and Fifth Symphonies provided Rachmaninov with a model for certain of his symphonic procedures.

The slow movement, an *adagio*, is as romantic as any music in the orchestral repertoire – if by romantic we mean the expression, through lyrical melody and richly chromatic harmony, of a sentiment which can only be described as love. The melody is almost always in the topmost voice – the 'right hand' of the orchestra – but this is not meant to imply that the music is conceived in pianistic terms; on the contrary, it would be impossible to make an effective piano transcription of it. But it would not be inappropriate to liken it to music for a great love scene in some romantic opera. In fact it does have quite a lot in common with the passionate love duet in Rachmaninov's own opera *Francesca da Rimini*.

The *adagio* opens with a short but very beautiful *ritornello* in which rising thirds, treated sequentially, play an important part:

Ex. 11

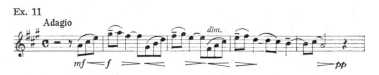

But the principal theme itself, announced by the solo clarinet, is the very epitome of Rachmaninov's most typical melodic style:

Ex. 12

It is a very long melody, moving mostly by step and never straying very far from the dominant of the scale – the note on which it begins. But though beautiful in itself it owes most of its poetic effect to the shifting and subtly organised harmonic web that underlies it. It could be thought that the restless elaboration of the accompaniment, with its constant subdivision of the strings, at times slightly overpowers the gentle, touching clarinet theme. But Rachmaninov has still richer delights in store, having held his first violins in reserve for a yet more emotionally ecstatic melodic outpouring which eventually culminates in the climactic return of the *ritornello* theme.

The central section of the *adagio* introduces a note of questioning into the music, much as lovers might demand from one another, as is their way, repeated assurances of undying affection. Here the violin figure from the symphony's motto theme reappears and plays an important part in the development of the music. The whole of this long section alternates what seems to be an interrogative phrase (perhaps it is 'Do you love me?', which happens to fit the music equally well in Russian),

Ex. 13

with ever more passionate avowals, eventually leading to yet another appearance of the *ritornello* theme.

The link between this climax and the return of the principal theme takes the form of a duet between the motto theme and the *ritornello* (scored mainly for solo violin and solo wind instruments), and when the long main theme is eventually restated the *ritornello*'s rising thirds are present, though remaining discreetly in the background, and add a sympathetic counterpoint to the passionate love music of the violins. In the coda the consoling phrases of the *ritornello* take precedence over all the other thematic material and bring this great nocturne-like piece to a conclusion in which, if all passion has not yet been completely spent, there is certainly a satisfactory feeling that 'twin souls' have been 'knit as one'. It is not surprising that the composer of this music should have been the object of much feminine adulation, not all of it expressed as unembarrassingly as the constant, though anonymous, floral tributes from one who was known to him only as 'the lady of the lilacs'.

The finale has about it a carnivalesque gaiety, which is not a mood one readily associates with Rachmaninov. Its opening bars, as has been mentioned, derive from a motif which had played an important part in the Scherzo:

Ex. 14

Other motifs from earlier movements, notably the motto theme and the questioning phrase from the slow movement, are also woven in among the whirling triplet figuration, with its suggestion of *saltarello* rhythm; but these reminiscences are introduced with infinitely greater skill than those in the finale of the First Symphony, and they do nothing to hinder the impetus of the music. In contrast to this activity there is yet another great flowing melody, played by the entire string orchestra less the double-basses. This is one of Rachmaninov's happiest inspirations in every sense, and it is, for him, an unusual theme in that it contains a great many intervals – very little of his characteristic step-wise movement.

Ex. 15

When in this optimistic *cantabile* vein, Rachmaninov seems able to spin out his melodic ideas to indefinite lengths, but eventually this beautiful theme gives place to a very brief *adagio* quotation from the slow movement before plunging once more into the seething activity of the dance.

There is now what is, in effect, a development section, in which occurs one of the most remarkable passages in all Rachmaninov's work. A descending scale in crotchets appears among the triplet movement and gradually assumes more and more importance until it is at last left unsupported but for a solo bassoon pedal on F. The descending scales then proliferate in every possible rhythmic variant – augmented, diminished, syncopated – and always louder.

It is as if a thousand bell-towers were ringing out a clamorous celebration of some great religious or national occasion. The sound of bells had a perennial fascination for Rachmaninov and was often echoed in his music, but in no other work, with the exception of his choral symphony *The Bells*, written a few years later, did he equal in originality and excitement this strange passage.

The recapitulation which follows immediately on the climax of the bell-like scales is predictable, though effectively scored. One is glad to hear again the great, optimistic string melody, rounded off this time with a short but sufficiently brilliant coda, and though one may perhaps think that the symphony has been brought to its conclusion in a somewhat labour-saving way it is also possible to take the view that to search for new aspects of the material for the end of so long a work would place too great a strain upon the receptiveness of an audience, even of one as attentive as that which enjoyed the first performance in St Petersburg in 1908.

SYMPHONY NO. 3 IN A MINOR, OP. 44

Rachmaninov's Third Symphony, though not his last important composition, dates from 1935–6, in the final phase of his career. It is one of his best works, and, though this was not recognised when it was first heard, it is also one of considerable originality. In this symphony the material is organised with such skill and economy that it would be impossible to make cuts in it like those sometimes made in his other symphonies, while its orchestration is throughout of the first order.

Rachmaninov was well aware that the symphony was one of his best works, and its lukewarm reception by the general public and cold rejection by the critics were both a disappointment and a puzzle to him. Doubtless the innumerable 'ordinary music-lovers' who revelled in the Second and Third Concertos and, when they had opportunities of hearing them, in *The Bells*, *The Isle of the Dead* and the Second Symphony, and who had recently taken to their hearts the *Rhapsody on a theme by Paganini* (mainly, one suspects, because its exciting pianism and luxuriantly romantic Eighteenth Variation deflected their attention from the dry wit and almost Prokofievian rhythmic drive of the larger part of that work) came to the first performance of the Third Symphony expecting something rather different from what they actually heard.

Unmindful of the hints of a changing style to be heard in the mis-understood Fourth Concerto of 1926 and in the still little-known *Etudes-Tableaux*, the public at the first London performance listened to the new symphony with surprise and with a slight sense of disappointment. It is true that the work was not helped on that occasion by the unsympathetic interpretation of Beecham, who rushed through the romantic second subject of the first movement with a relentless drive that typified his whole performance. Later performances by Sir Henry Wood were more idiomatic, but it was not until the composer's own recording with the Philadelphia Orchestra became generally available that the work's true value was revealed to those who were still prepared to listen to it without prejudice. As for the critics, it is difficult to understand what the critics of the thirties expected and required of Rachmaninov, then at the height of his fame as a pianist. Most of them seem positively to have resented the fact that he had composed a new symphony at all, and dire were their predictions of its early demise. For some time the work was little heard, and it seemed as if their prophecies were to be justified, but in recent years it has been played through-out the world with ever-increasing frequency (and nowhere more often than in Russia). Its future now seems reasonably safe.

Among those present at the first London performance was Rach-maninov's old friend and colleague Nikolai Medtner, who was as filled with eager expectation as anyone else in the crowded hall. And, sad to say, nobody was more disappointed than Medtner, though *his* distress was caused by what appeared to him to be Rach-maninov's concessions to 'modernism' in the symphony. Today it is as difficult to hear what these 'modernisms' are (they kept poor Medtner awake all night) as it is to understand the carpings of the critics, or, for that matter, the grumblings of those members of the general public whose own, rather different, expectations the sym-phony failed to match. So much time and music has come and gone (the latter mostly gone) since 1936 that we can now hear the work without worrying about what it is not but with a proper appreci-ation of what it is: and what we now hear is a vigorous, compact symphonic structure, scored with clarity and a wonderful feeling for subtle orchestral timbres.

The symphony is written with fastidious care and with an ele-gance of detail which demand close attention. It is not a simple piece in any sense, and it contains much that is unusual for Rachmaninov – a rather more adventurous harmonic range than that used for his earlier symphonies, great rhythmic freedom, various formal innovations (the telescoping of slow movement and Scherzo, if not without precedent, even among his own works, is achieved with admirable ease and certainty) and much dazzling orchestration, in which percussion instruments are used with notable resource. The care with which Rachmaninov blends his orchestral tone colours is evident in the very opening bars of the symphony, in which the motto (as in the other symphonies, a chant-like motto theme plays an important part in the plan of the work) is given out softly by the mingled tones of a solo horn, two clarinets and one muted cello:

Ex. 16

This fatalistic motif, with its narrow range of only three notes, seems at first to be almost too tentative, insufficiently memorable for the important role it has to play. Yet it is in fact carefully designed for its purpose, which is not so much to make dramatic, brassy intrusions (though on occasion it can do this to good effect) as to remind us, sometimes by no more than a quietly hinted reference, that our destiny is inescapable and that however persuasive human eloquence may be, fate will have the last, inevitable word. All very much in the Russian tradition. The motto theme once established, there is a moment of silence followed by a sudden rocketing scale, a few sonorously scored chords, and a bar or so of a pounding rhythm which serves to set the movement in motion. The real first subject, however, is a soft, hauntingly sad melody given out by the woodwind with an answering strain for the violins:

Ex. 17

The nostalgic atmosphere of this theme has been thought to be the expression of the exile's longing for his native land, though it is a mood which appears frequently in the work of other Russian artists, not necessarily exiles, and prevails in many of the plays of Chekhov, which Rachmaninov greatly admired.

The second subject, linked to the first by contrastingly animated material, is a broad, lyrical theme, heard first on the cellos. It is an example of Rachmaninov's most expansive and full-blooded style:

Ex. 18

This theme has been curiously described as 'a last fearful glance to the bygone days of the Second Concerto and Second Symphony',[1] which presumably means that it resembles the type of melody which Rachmaninov composed in the first decade of the century, though in what way it expresses trepidation it is impossible to understand. Certainly it is in his most romantic vein, and its rich scoring and increasingly fervent lyricism ultimately combine in a climax of great power. There is, of course, other important thematic material in the movement and, as has been mentioned, much interesting use of percussion instruments, including a xylophone which in one passage of whole-tone harmony is used in conjunction with piccolo and bassoon – a weird passage which was doubtless among those which so greatly agitated Medtner. Throughout the movement there is great rhythmic freedom; there are no *longueurs*, no miscalculations of scoring, everything is brought off with skill and complete conviction, and the movement ends, predictably, with a muttered reminder of the motto theme with which it opens.

It has already been pointed out that the second movement combines the elements of slow movement and Scherzo. Throughout the opening *adagio* section one is somehow aware that this is going to be no ordinary slow movement – that everything is as much designed to arouse expectation for what is to come as to touch the heart by beauty of sound. We hear first an entirely new thematic

[1] John Culshaw, *Sergei Rachmaninov* (London 1949).

metamorphosis of the motto theme, romantically scored for a solo
horn with rich, bardic accompanying chords for the harp, and this
is followed by a chain of important melodic elements: a descending sequence for solo violin; a rising melody for all the violins in
unison; a four-bar phrase for the flute which is given some development. But all of these, while interesting in themselves, never
continue for very long, and so the listener is partly prepared for
their eventual dissolution into a glittering shower of musical quick-
silver from which the principal theme of the Scherzo suddenly
appears on the scene:

Ex. 19

The word 'scene' is not one which has been lightly chosen, for it is
difficult not to suspect that, as in so many of Rachmaninov's ostensibly abstract compositions, some pictorial inspiration may well
have prompted this music, so vividly does it suggest the feverish
gaiety of a carnival picture by, perhaps, some such painter as Pieter
Breughel the Elder. Till Eulenspiegel himself seems to be cavorting
among laughing, protesting crowds in this riotous musical *Fasching*.
It is one of Rachmaninov's most vivacious and colourful pieces of
orchestral writing, and it is carried through with unflagging virtuosity. Even the difficult problem of how to return convincingly
from such a whirlwind of movement to the quiet poetry of the
adagio is satisfactorily solved. Two alternating violin trills on C
sharp and B, which, in a good performance, can sound like the toc-
sin of great alarm bells, break through the turmoil and then gradually still their vibrations until the music comes to rest on a held C
sharp . . . and from here it is an easy step to the gentle reintroduc-
tion of the various melodic ideas which formed the opening *adagio*.
These are now reset in such a way that the expectancy they formerly aroused is replaced by a feeling of nocturnal rapture, and in
this mood the movement might well have ended. But, as in the
first movement, we are again reminded, by another soft and rather
sinister allusion to the motto theme, that ours is a world of lost
illusions.

The mood of the last movement is one of brave defiance. Here is the opening subject:

It has great vitality and drive and succeeds by sheer technical virtuosity rather than by individually beautiful themes. Its most striking features are a splendid fugue, based on a transformation of the opening theme,

several short, lyrical themes which give relief to the prevailing motoric impetus, and the eventual introduction of a new motif – none other than Rachmaninov's old *idée fixe*, the 'Dies irae', which had already appeared in many of his other works. Whereas the motto theme makes only one important appearance, just before the brilliant fugal section, the 'Dies irae' haunts the whole of the later part of the finale. The motto is present, however, in a disguised form, in the coda, where it underlies the flute solo which begins the *allegretto* section:

The last pages of the symphony are as colourful and as rhythmically vivid as was Rachmaninov's piano playing, and nothing was ever more exciting than that. The work is indeed a virtuoso piece, written for and inspired by virtuoso performers, in this case the members of the Philadelphia Orchestra. This fact undoubtedly dictated, to some extent, the form and character of the symphony and the brilliant orchestral style adopted by the composer. That it is not as rich in long, romantic melodies as some of his earlier large-scale works is a sign not of waning powers but of a different emphasis, a different intention, which was the outcome of a gradual slight shift of his values in composition. Rachmaninov perfectly succeeded in what he set out to do in this symphony, and orchestras and conductors are evidently becoming increasingly aware of its importance as a valuable addition to the symphonic repertoire of the twentieth century.

Works for Piano and Orchestra

CONCERTO NO. 1 IN F SHARP MINOR, OP. 1

This work exists in two widely different published versions. The earlier version was written in 1891, when Rachmaninov was only eighteen. Its first movement was performed at a students' concert of the Moscow Conservatoire on 17 March 1892, with the composer as soloist and the formidable director of the conservatoire, V. I. Safonov, as conductor. The programme was of mammoth proportions and included many concertos, concerto movements and arias played and sung by the principal graduates of the year. Rachmaninov's work was played in the middle of the concert, and a fellow student, who was a member of the orchestra, recalled how the composer resisted Safonov's proposed 'improvements' to his score during the rehearsals, and how he even daringly criticised the conductor's tempo – a clear indication that he was then full of confidence in his talent, for he was in Safonov's bad books at the time.

Through the influence of Tchaikovsky, on whom Rachmaninov's opera *Aleko* had made a very favourable impression, the fortunate young composer received, in 1893, a valuable contract from the Moscow publisher Gutheil, as a result of which not only *Aleko* but also the First Concerto and all Rachmaninov's other early works (including the Prelude in C sharp minor) were printed as soon as composed. The concerto appeared as Opus 1. However, despite this promising start the First Concerto does not seem to have been played with any frequency in its original form, and Rachmaninov himself soon regretted its premature publication. As his talent developed he became aware that the concerto lacked technical polish; that despite charming melodic material, its formal and textural defects were serious enough to prevent it from becoming an established part of the repertoire; and that with the work already in print the only way of salvaging it would be to republish it in a revised version which would supersede the original.

Rachmaninov had this intention in mind for some time (he mentioned it in a letter to a friend written in 1908), but it was not until many years later, when his Second and Third Concertos had scored triumphant successes throughout Europe and America, that he found time to revise his Concerto in F sharp minor. He chose what seems a strange moment to set about the task. In September 1917, when Russia was in a state of frightful turmoil, he left his country estate, Ivanovka, where, during the summer, he had experienced some uncomfortable encounters with local Bolshevist agitators, and moved to his flat in Moscow, ostensibly in preparation for the winter concert season. There, living curiously isolated from the world-shattering events which were taking place around him, he set about the revision of his youthful concerto, and very soon became so absorbed in the work that he hardly noticed the sinister crackle of rifle fire in the streets outside. At this same time he made some sketches for a new concerto which was eventually to become his Fourth, in G minor, but the revision of the First Concerto was the last work which he completed in Russia, apart from three small piano pieces which were composed a few days after the manuscript of the concerto had been delivered to Gutheil's publishing house.

Rachmaninov was rightly pleased with the First Concerto in its new form, and it was a disappointment to him that throughout his pianistic career his fans continued to demand his other concertos in preference to it. It certainly deserves the attention which nowadays it receives in fair measure, for though a shorter and somewhat lighter work than its famous successors it is equally brilliant and full of melodic charm. Rachmaninov's revisions were extremely drastic. Not only did he give the original material new and improved presentation, but he reworked it in infinitely more subtle ways than formerly, clarified the orchestration, and recast the solo part in such a manner that it demands the utmost panache and bravura from the pianist. A great cadenza plays an important part in the first movement, occupying more than a quarter of its length. This cadenza brings to a final climax all the principal material and makes striking use not only of the two leading themes, but also of the fateful trumpet call with which the work begins and of the solo passage in octaves which immediately succeeds it, this last being no mere piece of empty display but an important element in the structure of the piece.

The slow movement needed much less revision, and its charming theme, presented by the soloist without accompaniment, remained virtually unchanged. It has something of the character, and also the dimensions, of a Chopin nocturne, but it is Chopin filtered through the works of Tchaikovsky and Arensky, who were the two principal influences on Rachmaninov in his early years. The haunting melody of the opening is eventually taken up by the orchestra while the piano continues with a richly decorative accompaniment which enhances but does not disturb the music's calm, moonlit romanticism.

The finale, which in its original form seems to have been modelled on that of Grieg's Concerto in A minor (a work much admired by Rachmaninov, who, however, never played the solo part in public, though he once conducted it with his cousin, Alexander Siloti, as soloist), was the movement to which he gave the most drastic revision, both its form and its texture being entirely reworked from beginning to end. Though no new themes were introduced, every bar was improved in detail, much was omitted, and in the greatly revised passage-work there is often a reflection of the more advanced harmonic manner which Rachmaninov had developed in his later Preludes and *Etudes-Tableaux*. Yet the capricious, dancing gaiety of the gypsy-like principal theme is in no way spoiled by the new sophistication of its presentation. The most important alteration to the piece concerns the romantically beautiful theme in E flat major, marked *andante ma non troppo,* which forms the central episode of the movement. This melody is presented by the strings with a decorative commentary from the piano at the end of each phrase. In the original version these decorations were little more than freely improvised 'cascades', but in the revision they become echoes, in diminution, of the theme itself. The development of the theme and its eventual restatement are given to the piano, the orchestra taking over the quasi-canonic echoes, and the whole episode ends quietly in much the same way as the F major episode in the finale of Grieg's concerto. But whereas in his first version Rachmaninov rounded off his finale (as did Grieg) with a grandiose restatement of the *andante* theme by the orchestra, accompanied by a sonorous piano part, in the revised version the work is brought to an end in a blaze of dancing virtuosity, à la Trepak, the E flat *andante* thus being relegated to the status of an isolated episode, like a beautiful miniature portrait in a glittering, jewelled setting. It is a possibility that the composer's innumerable admirers, attuned to the soaringly ecstatic conclusions of his Second and Third Concertos, might have succumbed more quickly to the undoubted charms of the Concerto in F sharp minor had he allowed them (as had been his original intention) a final, glorified vision of the *andante* melody before rounding off the work with a suitably exciting coda. This, of course, is mere conjecture, and one must be glad that Rachmaninov found the time and opportunity in his busy life to revise this early work so thoroughly that it has become a valuable addition to the piano concerto repertoire. He might never have done so had he not been in need of an absorbing occupation at a time when the flow of ideas for original composition had been halted by the anxieties and uncertainties of life in a country in the first throes of revolution.

CONCERTO NO. 2 IN C MINOR, OP. 18

The Second Concerto is in many ways the most important work in Rachmaninov's career as a composer. It marks a turning-point in his life, and its immediate and extraordinary success reaffirmed to the composer himself, as well as to his public, the strength and value of his creative talent.

Most people know the story of how, depressed by the disastrous failure of his First Symphony, the young composer sank into a state of apathy and found himself unable to compose, or at all events lost interest in composition for many months; how his relations, the Satin family, having tried on him all the more usual cures for nervous depression, finally persuaded him to submit to the treatment of Dr Nikolai Dahl, a practitioner of medical hypnosis who had already successfully treated Rachmaninov's aunt, Varvara Satina, for what would now be regarded as a nervous illness of psychosomatic origin. It is likely that it was the success of Dr Dahl's treatment of Madame Satina which gave Rachmaninov confidence in him, and it is probable that by good luck (for this is always a matter of chance) the young man happened to be what is called in medicohypnosis terms an 'amnesic' type, and therefore susceptible to suggestion under hypnosis. Be that as it may, after a series of relaxing sessions with Dr Dahl Rachmaninov began to write his new concerto quite easily, and soon found that his inspiration, which had been dammed up for nearly three years, was once more freely flowing with good melodic ideas, far more indeed than he needed for a single work. It is all the more curious, therefore, that the actual starting-point of his work on the Second Concerto was not one of the abundance of new themes produced by his reawakened creative urge, but a reminiscence of something which he had composed long before.

In 1890 Rachmaninov had enjoyed an intimate friendship with a family named Skalon, distant relations of his own, and he had composed for the three Skalon daughters two pieces for the unusual combination of six hands on one keyboard. The second of these two pieces, a *Romance*, begins with the following passage, played by the *terzo* part of the Trio:

Ex. 23
Andante sostenuto

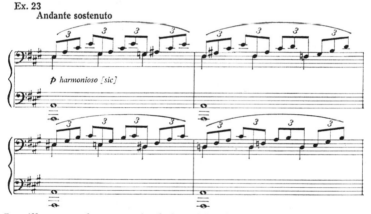

It will at once be recognised that this, though but an accompaniment figuration and not a melody, is the very essence of the slow movement of the Second Concerto, and it was with this part of the work and not the first movement (which was written last) that Rachmaninov began his new concerto. In the *Romance* written for the Skalon girls the passage introduces a different melody from that of the concerto, and it is, of course, in another key; nevertheless it is this passage, with its interesting rhythmic ambiguity, which is really the vitalising element in the concerto's slow movement, and it was from this seed, sown ten years previously but since then lying fallow, that the glowing Second Concerto was eventually to come to fruition.

There is another important theme in the concerto which is also derived from part of an earlier work which Rachmaninov had discarded. One would scarcely have supposed that the scintillating principal subject of the finale, an idea which seems to have been born under the virtuoso's flying fingers, could have even the remotest connection with music originally composed for the Russian church, yet such is the case. In 1893 Rachmaninov had composed a short sacred concerto for four-part choir (the so-called 'sacred' or 'spiritual concerto' for chorus, *a cappella,* is a distinctive feature of Orthodox Church music) which, though modelled on those of Bortnyansky, who wrote many such works, is quite personal in idiom and touchingly beautiful. It was performed by the Moscow Synodical Choir in December 1893, but it was not heard again in the composer's lifetime and it remained unpublished until 1955. Its first section proves to be largely based on a motif which is identical with that of the finale of the Second Concerto, as is illustrated by the following passage from it:

Ex. 24

Once launched on his work, Rachmaninov's former apathy disappeared; the second and third movements of the concerto were quickly completed, other new works were begun, and a somewhat risky project, the public performance of the concerto in its incomplete state, was undertaken, apparently without a qualm. Rachmaninov played the slow movement and finale at a charity concert in 1900, and it scored an overwhelming success with the public and critics alike. It was all he needed to complete his cure, and the concerto, too, was soon complete, its first movement being written early in 1901.

The work is now too familiar to need elaborate analysis or quotation, but the following points must be mentioned. It has been stated that the celebrated second theme of the finale is not an original melody by Rachmaninov but that it was 'given' to him (on request) by his old fellow-pupil, M. Pressman. This statement was first made by the late L. Sabaneyev, and is mentioned in Viktor Seroff's biography of Rachmaninov: it is difficult to accept. Until more definite proof than a statement repeated at third-hand can be produced one can remain sceptical of the possibility that this celebrated and memorable tune, so typical of Rachmaninov at the height of his powers, was really the work of one of his colleagues – a colleague, moreover, who is not known to have written anything else of importance, and who, though a very gifted pianist, was decidedly academic in his general outlook on music. Whether one likes the theme or not (and there are those who do not) is beside the point.

The resounding success of the incomplete concerto not only enhanced Rachmaninov's status in Moscow's musical world; it also aroused excited interest in how the work would be completed. Which brings us to the curious fact that the now well-known first theme of the first movement appears to stem from a relatively unimportant linking passage in the finale:

Ex. 25

The bass figure marked *x* may well have given rise to the opening phrase of the first movement's violin theme (it is in such ways that the creative mind works, sometimes consciously but more often subconsciously), but had the first movement been composed before the last the motif *x* would certainly be pointed out as a deliberate quotation from the first movement.

One of the most original features of the Second Concerto is its opening – the chain of alternating chords and deep bass notes for the piano, beginning softly in F minor but swelling to an enormous volume of sound as the harmony shifts about semitonally towards a final resolution into the real tonic, C minor (a passage which, incidentally, bears a curious likeness to the conclusion of the notorious C sharp minor Prelude, but seen, as it were, in reverse). This introduction is now so familiar that one takes it for granted and forgets too easily its novelty in 1901.

Another curious feature of the first movement is that the solo

47

part is largely accompanimental or decorative, the burden of melody remaining with the orchestra to a very great extent. Indeed, the orchestra is silent less often than the soloist, and, unlike its neighbours among Rachmaninov's concertos, the Second has no first-movement cadenza in which the soloist's virtuosity can be unleashed and exploited to the full: nevertheless the work is difficult, both technically and musically, demanding brilliant pianism as well as the musicianship and finesse of an experienced chamber-music player who is prepared both to listen and to lead. Rachmaninov himself once said that his Second Concerto is more 'uncomfortable' to play than his Third. This is a statement with which few professional pianists will agree, but he probably had in mind this very matter of close integration between piano and orchestra and the need for absolute rhythmic security (the fugato passage in the finale is a pitfall in this respect) rather than the degree of pianistic virtuosity required.

It is not generally realised that the Second Concerto is the first orchestral work which Rachmaninov wrote after the débâcle of the first (and, in his lifetime, only) performance of his First Symphony. In effectiveness of orchestration the concerto is a great advance on the sometimes turgid textures of the symphony, and though the score does not yet show the mastery of colour and, in particular, the skill in the use of percussion instruments which are evident in his later works, one should not miss such a delicate touch as the soft cymbal clashes which add spice to the orchestral chords punctuating the piano's triplet melody in the *meno mosso* sections of the finale. It is such felicitous details as this, as well as its abundance of heartfelt melody, its complete sincerity and its masterly construction, which confound those unsympathetic critics who periodically foretell its disappearance from the repertoire, and which earn it the place it continues to hold in the affection of an ever-widening public. After seventy years it is still one of the best-loved pieces of music ever written.

CONCERTO NO. 3 IN D MINOR, OP. 30

During the earlier years of its existence this now extremely popular concerto was seldom performed. This was not because it lacked any of those notable qualities – romantic melody, virtuoso piano-writing, exciting rhythms – which had at once placed the Second

Concerto among the first half dozen of the world's most beloved piano concertos, but because the sheer physical staying power and digital brilliance needed for an adequate performance of it were too demanding for all but a few pianists of the time. Rachmaninov's own playing of the work set a standard other pianists rarely cared to challenge. (Even its dedicatee, Josef Hofmann, considered by Rachmaninov the greatest pianist of the day, never essayed it.) It was not until the 1930s that the extraordinary mastery of piano-playing (mastery which encompasses every sublety of tone-gradation and pedalling as well as formidable manual dexterity and untiring muscles) found adequate representation in such pianists as Vladimir Horowitz, the short-lived Alexander Helman, Walter Gieseking (whose amazing performance of the concerto Rachmaninov admired more than any others), and later some of the younger pianists of the British and Soviet schools. Even today it remains a testing undertaking, but with a new race of virtuosi who can meet this trial of strength and emerge from the experience unscathed, the Third Concerto is now almost as frequently played as the Second.

The opening of the first movement is of a deceptive simplicity. It is merely a long melody played by the soloist in octaves, one note to each hand; a theme which seldom moves far from the tonic but which, once heard, is not easily forgotten; a curious theme, essentially Russian yet of universal appeal. It is not surprising that Rachmaninov was often asked if it was a folk melody, or if it perhaps derived from one of those ancient church chants which he was known to have used in several other works.

Ex. 26

We may be sure that he was quite sincere when he denied any such origin for his theme. Indeed, he always maintained that he had not consciously composed it, but that it had 'created itself'. However, the researches of the musicologist Joseph Yasser have, since Rachmaninov's death, drawn attention to some very remarkable similarities between the concerto's main theme and that of an old Russian monastic chant, 'Thy tomb, O Saviour, soldiers guarding':

Ex. 27

The likeness between these two themes is sufficiently striking for it to be possible that Rachmaninov, perhaps during his frequent boyhood visits with his grandmother to the monastic churches of the Novgorod region, heard the old chant and stored it away in his subconscious musical memory until it rose to the surface, transmogrified into its present form, when he began to compose the Third Concerto. The fact that he felt that the theme came to him 'ready made' adds some support to this theory.

But if the principal theme came by itself, its accompaniment certainly did not. Rachmaninov had considerable difficulty in finding the right kind of background for the theme, one which would throb with life yet not distract attention from the piano's simple melody. The accompaniment's pattern is in fact important in itself as material for development, and later it is used climactically with excellent effect. As soon as the soloist completes the theme he changes place with the orchestra. The melody is now repeated by the strings while the piano continues with semiquaver figuration derived from the accompanying harmonies. Certainly this passage is marked *più mosso,* but it is a pity that soloists and conductors larely agree about the actual change of speed. Too often the pianist flies ahead, unconcerned about the orchestra's melodic line, and leaving the conductor to keep up with him as best he can; and too often the conductor fails to do so.

The second subject falls into two parts: the first a conversational exchange between piano and orchestra; the second a romantic *cantabile* melody presented mainly as a piano solo, though not without some discreet orchestral backing. The development section, mainly derived from the first theme, is followed by a series of sequential patterns that lead to what is a very important formal innovation – the replacement of the normal recapitulation by an enormous and very difficult cadenza. This is no ordinary cadenza but an essential part of the structure, providing it with the necessary element of repetition. Rachmaninov actually wrote two alternative cadenzas, one even more exacting to play than the other, but they both follow much the same path and coalesce into the same music about half-way through. The movement ends with a short coda which begins with an exact restatement of the opening theme in its original form and is then neatly rounded off with a brief reference to the conversational exchange of the first part of the second subject.

The second movement, an *adagio* entitled 'Intermezzo', is largely based on a poetic melody which grows out of a falling phrase played by the violins in the very first bar. This melody, which is developed orchestrally in music of an elegiac beauty, has many latent possibilities, as the soloist soon gets an opportunity to reveal. The extraordinary piano entry, a sudden wild intrusion, has a dual purpose: to end brusquely the wistful mood of the orchestral prelude, and to break up its key centre (A major) and draw the music, by a complex web of chromatic lines, towards what is the true key of the Intermezzo, D flat major – an unusual key for the slow movement of a concerto in D minor. The soloist is now fully in command, and, having established the key, he proceeds to present his own version of the main theme, richly harmonised and laid out with a lavish sumptuousness of tone, and then, in the pages which follow, to derive from the same initial falling phrase a great stream of melody such as Rachmaninov himself rarely matches elsewhere in his work. It is curious how the key of D flat has inspired many composers of piano music to a peculiarly luxuriant romanticism: Chopin, Liszt, Grieg, Debussy and Skryabin all felt its lure, which may indeed have a definite physical origin in the sensuous 'feel' of this tonality under the pianist's fingers. Rachmaninov was to return to it for similar music in later works.

During the soloist's long exposition of the principal theme the orchestra assumes a mainly accompanying role, though there is one moment when sharp ears may hear a reminder from the violins that the theme of the first movement has still to be reckoned with. It would have been easy enough to have simply rounded off the *adagio,* once the piano's great rhapsodic outburst has been completed, with a return to the music of the opening; and indeed something of the kind does eventually occur, but not before an entirely new section, in the form of a lilting waltz in F sharp minor, its theme a rhythmic variant of the first movement theme hinted at a little earlier in the movement, has been introduced. The melodic line of this interlude is given to the orchestra, the piano decorating it with coruscating triplet figurations which need more discreet handling than they usually get if they are not to blot out the delicate scoring of the melody. The interpolation of this waltz may have been an afterthought (it is not, however, one of the various cuts in the concerto which were misguidedly authorised by the composer), for it leads back to the key of D flat, now enharmonically changed to C sharp, and to the main theme of the *adagio*. Here the orchestra allows the soloist a much-needed rest, during a reprise of the opening in a rescoring for wind which lends it a grandeur that is, in its simplicity, an effective contrast to the rich elaboration of the bulk of the movement. This orchestral coda is interrupted by the soloist with a dramatic bravura passage which serves both as a link to the finale and a convincing modulation from C sharp back to the 'home' key of D minor.

The finale is one of the most dashing and exciting pieces of music ever composed for piano and orchestra. Every possibility of the modern piano is exploited in it: the impetuous opening theme in D minor; the rhythmically urgent theme in C and its variant, the happy, soaring melody in G – all are carried forward on wave after wave of dazzling passage-work, backed by an ever-widening range of pianistic resonances, by Rachmaninov's characteristic rhythmic verve, and by effective orchestration. The most difficult structural problem of the movement (how to provide relief and contrast to such an opening without allowing the interest to sag) is solved with skill. The exposition of the principal themes is followed by a long central episode consisting of what is really a short set of variations on a capricious, light-footed theme which, though it seems at first to be unrelated to earlier material, proves, on analysis, to derive from the opening theme of the finale and the second subject of the first movement. This central section is all poised over an E flat pedal, the piano performing its daring acrobatic marvels over a soft cushion of string tone. There are four of these miniature variations, each more fascinatingly ornate than the last, but between the second and third there is a short interlude in which both the principal subjects of the first movement are recalled, only to be thrust aside as the soloist resumes his dare-devil feats of tight-rope virtuosity. This central episode concludes with a roll for timpani and a few cadential chords for the piano which end with a full close in E flat.

The themes of the first section then reappear, all of them a tone lower than before and all presented in entirely different ways. The happy G major theme, now in F, is extended until the key of D minor has been re-established; and then, with an ever-increasing excitement, a long and percussive coda on a dominant pedal leads, via a tempestuous cascade of piano octaves, to a final ecstatic outburst of melody from both piano and orchestra, obviously derived from, but not identical with, the third main subject of the movement. Into this long and effective coda Rachmaninov put all that he had in reserve of glamour and excitement, for the summing-up of so brilliant and so emotionally high-powered a concerto was in itself a challenge not to be shirked. The Third Concerto, as a consequence, is the ultimate in romantic virtuoso pieces – the kind of work which it would be extremely difficult to follow with another essay in the same manner. Rachmaninov must have been very conscious of this. He must have realised that in his next concerto, should he ever write another, he would have to adopt quite a different approach to the form, and that in following a completely unfamiliar path he might meet pitfalls which would be difficult to negotiate. It was perhaps for this reason that so many years elapsed between the composition of the Third Concerto and its successor, and that when the Fourth Concerto appeared it caused surprise and failed to please admirers of the earlier concertos. It is, however, an interesting if not wholly successful work and it has gained some ground in recent years. But it is never likely to achieve the popularity with both public and performers of its more celebrated predecessors.

CONCERTO NO. 4 IN G MINOR, OP. 40

According to the composer, it was his work on the revision of his First Concerto which prompted him to begin his Concerto in G minor. The earliest sketches for this work, therefore, date from 1917, though the greater part of it was written long afterwards. The score was completed in August 1926, and the first performance took place in Philadelphia (not in Berlin, as is sometimes stated) the following year. It proved a dismal failure with both the public and the critics, and though Rachmaninov played it in Europe and America for a few more seasons, and even allowed it to be printed, it was not taken up by other pianists until after its drastic revision in 1941. The composer seems to have had some doubts about it even before its first performance, for in an interesting correspondence with Nikolai Medtner, to whom it is dedicated, he mentioned his fear that the concerto might prove to be too long. Yet it is in fact by no means long, and it is strange that Rachmaninov did not recognise how concise are its proportions (even in its unrevised form) compared with those of the Third or even the Second Concertos. He also worried about the theme of the slow movement, once he had observed that it somewhat resembled the opening theme of Schumann's Piano Concerto. Unkind critics of the Fourth Concerto have never failed to point out that it sounds even more like the old nursery-rhyme tune 'Three Blind Mice', though, oddly enough, Schumann's concerto has not had to endure the same mockery.

The first movement opens with a long melody which combines a characteristically Rachmaninovian mixture of energy and pessimism. This theme almost certainly dates from 1917, and is doubtless a reflection of the composer's state of mind during that last anxious autumn in Russia. An unusual feature of the theme is its scoring: it is given out in full-handed chords by the piano, supported by a rich, vibrant orchestral accompaniment – the kind of layout which Rachmaninov had, in the past, reserved for the great climaxes and codas of his concertos. The second subject is a charming but rather light-weight melody over which the piano and woodwind indulge in gentle conversational exchanges, but this theme proves to be of less ultimate importance than a tiny, leaping figure which immediately succeeds it:

Ex. 28

This little motif, heard first on a solo bassoon, is eventually to become the leading theme of the finale. But the actual thematic material is, on the whole, of less intrinsic interest than the change in Rachmaninov's idiom evident in the larger part of the movement. There is, of course, no stylistic *volte-face*: the old Rachmaninov is still perfectly recognisable. Nevertheless, there is a new rhythmic freedom, an occasional harmonic harshness (the frequent use of consecutive fifths would not have pleased Rachmaninov's harmony teacher Arensky), and above all an increased resource in the orchestration that points the way to the Third Symphony and the *Symphonic Dances*.

The two principal themes are heard in reverse order in the recapitulation, the long first subject, originally presented in strong piano chords, now soaring high on violins supported by rippling arpeggios from the piano. This passage is splendidly conceived. But a stumbling-block, even to Rachmaninov's most fanatical admirers, has always been the short and strangely brusque coda, a mere six bars of impatient, syncopated chords which brutally dismiss the nostalgic romanticism of the pages immediately preceding them. This coda met with strong protest from contemporary critics, who unanimously condemned it. Yet it must have exactly carried out its composer's intentions, since he left it unchanged when he drastically revised the concerto many years later.

Those who expect a Rachmaninov slow movement to sound something like a glorified Chopin nocturne will be disappointed by the strangely austere *largo* of the Fourth Concerto. It is, for the most part, very simple in texture, and Medtner was probably right when he suggested that it might have some extra-musical inspiration, such as a solemn religious procession. Rachmaninov freely admitted that he was often inspired by a picture or a poem, though he usually kept these sources of his inspiration a close secret. In the present case we have very little more to go on than Medtner's imaginative idea, though there is a clue in the fact that an actual connection exists between this *largo* and one of Rachmaninov's *Etudes-Tableaux*. When he published his first set of pieces with this title he withheld the third of the set, in C minor. It was eventually published several years after his death, and it was at once clear that he had made good use of the beautiful concluding pages of the suppressed *Etude* in the slow movement of his Fourth Concerto.

Like that of the Third Concerto, this slow movement is linked to the finale. There is, in fact, a close connection between the falling minor second in the last bars of the *largo* and the opening bars of the *allegro vivace*, and this interval, furthermore, proves to be an important element in the principal theme of the finale. As we have seen, the theme is developed from the little four-note motif heard in the first movement (Ex. 27) – another instance of Rachmaninov's concern for unity in his larger works, in many of which the cyclic principle is a dominating factor.

Though the first two movements of the concerto offer few severe technical problems for the soloist, in the finale matters are quite otherwise. While not demanding the extreme of virtuosity and physical endurance required by the finale of the Third Concerto it is, nevertheless, a very difficult piece to play, not least in its rapid changes from moments of glittering display to passages in which the solo part, while no less difficult, becomes so integrated with the orchestra that it is necessary for the pianist quickly to adopt an entirely different approach to his task. This was the movement to which Rachmaninov made the most extensive changes when he revised the concerto. The central episode, in which a fanfare-like motif in triplets, alternating with romantic phrases for solo horn, suddenly flowers into a poetic, lyrical passage in Rachmaninov's earlier manner (the key here is, significantly, D flat), was quite recast, as was the larger part of the very percussive final section. Into this (in the revised version only) an important quotation from the first movement is introduced and slightly developed in a further attempt to give the work greater unity. It must be admitted that though the finale is not abnormally long it is not without some *longueurs,* and this last section in particular sometimes seems to lack direction. But as a whole it is an interesting piece in its rhythmic freedom, its clear and colourful orchestration and not least in the atmosphere of sardonic, and occasionally macabre, humour which, first appearing in this work, was to become an important element in Rachmaninov's final and in some ways most perfect work for piano and orchestra, the *Rhapsody on a theme by Paganini.*

RHAPSODY ON A THEME BY PAGANINI, OP. 43

This work is one of Rachmaninov's masterpieces. Its form is admirably planned, its scoring a triumph of skill, and its solo part as rewarding to play as to hear; added to which it has wit, charm, more than a dash of romance, and an unfailing rhythmic excitement. Even people who dislike Rachmaninov's music in general are known to admire this work: they cannot, in honesty, deny the originality of its conception or its brilliantly successful execution.

If Rachmaninov felt that he had suffered a fiasco in the cold reception accorded to his Fourth Concerto in 1927 (partly offset, it is true, by the success of his *Three Russian Songs* for chorus and orchestra, Op. 41) he had recovered from it by 1931, when he wrote his *Variations on a theme by Corelli.* So when he came in 1934 to compose the *Rhapsody on a theme by Paganini,* he was obviously full of self-confidence. The very fact that he could foresee so many possibilities in a tune which, one might have thought, had already been squeezed dry by Brahms and Liszt, to say nothing of Paganini is sufficient indication of this.

It is likely that the idea of the fascinating and highly original ballet which Fokine choreographed to this music in 1939 may have been in Rachmaninov's mind from the first, for the ballet's scenario was provided by the composer himself, and, as has been said, he often found a stimulus in some concealed pictorial or dramatic programme. The very ghost of Paganini – pale, angular, emaciated – is conjured up for us by the masterly opening of the work, in which the theme is anticipated by a 'skeletonised' version of it – a trimmed-down outline which is played by the orchestra and then used by the piano to add bony edges to the theme itself, first announced, appropriately enough, by all the violins in unison. There are in fact hints of Paganini's own treatment of the theme in the first six of Rachmaninov's variations, in which the interplay between piano and orchestra remains always in strict tempo. But in variation 7 there appears for the first time a different theme, none other than that old funeral chant, the 'Dies irae', which plays so important a part in Rachmaninov's work. The tempo now changes to *moderato* while the piano plays the chant in simple, solemn harmonies, the orchestra adding both augmented and diminished fragments of the Paganini theme in the background. From time to time throughout the work the 'Dies irae' reappears, always with dramatic effect, but it must not be supposed that the *Rhapsody* now becomes a set of variations on two themes of equal importance. Paganini's theme always remains the essence of the music, and in variation 8, which resumes the tempo of the opening, its harmonic framework still underlies Rachmaninov's ever-inventive treatment of its by now familiar melodic figures.

Variation 9 is less concerned with the development of the theme than with an intensification of its inherently demoniac character. To achieve this Rachmaninov combines such effects as the spectral rattle of strings playing with the wood of their bows, and the dry tapping of a side-drum, with a nervous, off-beat piano part which twice culminates in an agitated clatter of descending triplets played two octaves apart. The uncanny atmosphere thus created also pervades variation 10, which begins as a grotesque march that might almost be by Prokofiev. Here the bass line is derived from the 'Dies irae' while the piano thunders out the same theme in slow octaves, like the knell of great bells. In the central part of the variation the chant is jerked about rhythmically in a positively blasphemous manner, and when the march returns it appears high up on harp, piano (left hand) and glockenspiel, while the pianist's right hand adds a figuration derived from the Paganini theme. This satirical music is followed by a kind of improvisation (variation 11), which is also a cadenza for the soloist, with an important part for the harp, serving to release the music from the key of A minor to which it has so far been firmly attached.

There is now a section of much greater tonal freedom. First come two variations in D minor, one a graceful, pensive minuet, the other a vigorous *allegro* in which a new version of Paganini's theme, in 3/4 time, is given out by the full string orchestra while the piano accompanies with heavy chords and octaves. Then follow a pair of related variations in F major. In the first of these (variation 14) the vivacious, stimulating melodic line is allotted to the orchestra (first to the violins and woodwind and later to the brass), the piano being relegated to a still more subsidiary role than in the previous variation. Indeed, out of the thirty-seven bars of variation 14 the piano is essential in only twelve, which appears to have caused Rachmaninov to have second thoughts since he added to his orchestration of the central part twelve optional bars for the piano – an option which no performer of the *Rhapsody* has, so far, failed to take up. Variation 15, on the other hand, though closely related to its predecessor, places the soloist very much to the fore, half of it being entirely unaccompanied and the rest only lightly supported by the orchestra.

After a short pause the music shifts to B flat minor for a variation in 2/4, marked *allegretto*, which is scored with an exquisite chamber-music-like delicacy. Phrases for solo oboe, horn, violin, clarinet, and cor anglais are interwoven with a fine-spun accompaniment mostly scored for piano, plucked strings and harp, and have as their most noticeable feature a figure derived from the first two bars of Paganini's theme:

Ex. 29

In variation 17, the last three notes of this same motif, softly given out by the brass, and later the woodwind, are all that is left to remind us of Paganini. The music here seems to be stirring uneasily, as if groping its way through dark catacombs of modulation, until it eventually emerges into that key of sunset and romance, D flat major.

The now-celebrated eighteenth variation is a remarkable illustration of how easily Rachmaninov could, when he would, return to his most popular style. Merely by twisting the initial phrase of Paganini's theme upside-down a stream of romantic melody and harmony gushes forth with a warmth and naturalness which is quite equal to any of Rachmaninov's earlier melodic inspirations. After the pianist has stated the theme as a solo it is immediately taken up by the violins and cellos, with a lavish piano accompaniment, this second statement being followed by a third in which the strings soar yet more ecstatically, while the piano, backed by the harp, supports them with an even richer harmonic texture. But of course Rachmaninov has not been content to give us three identical presentations of the well-known melody, for exact repetition of the line never extends beyond the fourth bar; in each case the theme pursues a different course, the last leading to a coda, based on a tonic pedal, in which the soloist rounds off the piece with a series of soft, valedictory echoes of the inverted Paganini motif with which it began.

Variations 19 to 24 together form a finale in which the basic key is, once again, A minor. The legendary playing of Paganini, with its incredible left-hand pizzicato, lies behind variation 19, while the uncanny, satanic tales associated with him are perhaps suggested in variations 20 and 21. In variation 22 we seem to hear a hallucinatory *Marche au supplice* (the descending bass passages are said to have been suggested to Rachmaninov by a piece called *Parade* by the American composer Abram Chasins), and here the 'Dies irae' adds its fateful tones to the nightmarish crescendo which is built up over a long tonic pedal, only to become lost in the seething whirlpool of modulatory arpeggios, scales and cadenzas from which the piano eventually emerges with the theme now presented, somewhat surprisingly, in A flat minor. But this key the orchestra cannot tolerate, and the soloist is dragged unceremoniously back into A minor for a rhythmically exciting penultimate variation which leads, via thunderous octave scales, explosive orchestral interjections, and a soaring flight by the soloist from one end of the keyboard to the other, to the final, ultra-brilliant variation which, though it begins at a reduced tempo, soon gathers speed and culminates in a deliberately crude intrusion of the 'Dies irae', blared out by the full orchestra in a series of chords in root position. The terrifying old chant might very easily have been allowed the last word, but the conclusion of this unique work is as unusual as it is witty: the piece ends, not with the crash of bravura, but with a last mocking snatch of Paganini's theme over two soft, crisp, cadential chords.

Rachmaninov was sixty-one when he wrote his *Rhapsody*, a truth that is too frequently forgotten by those who seek to prove that his separation from his homeland not only caused him great personal sorrow but also stultified his creative powers. This work shows them at their height.

Index

DATE DUE			